MANUFACTURING WITH *Heart*

13 Employee-Centric Actions to Unlock Profitability

by

Loyal Peterman and Tanya Patrella

13 Employee-Centric Actions to Unlock Profitability

Published by:

Manufacturing with Heart, Inc.
5475 Lake Shore Avenue
Westerville, OH 43082
www.manufacturingwithheart.com

Cover and Interior design: Randy Wood

ISBN: 978-0-9971584-0-3

Library of Congress Control Number: 2015960985

Printed in the United States of America

From our hearts to yours…

Contents

Introduction

Manufacturers today need significant improvements in profitability and productivity. They need to reduce internal scrap and returned product. They need to reduce turnover, attract skilled employees and have them more involved in daily decision-making, more collaborative and more accountable. They need an agile and innovative environment. Corporations spend millions of dollars on capital equipment and leadership training to improve productivity and profitability, while the largest expense and greatest potential for improvement goes wanting… employees. To release that potential, it is essential to transition from a limiting focus on plant, capital, lean and metrics to earn the hands, minds and hearts of employees.

For years organizations have developed an ever-increasing set of rules and policies that are designed to manage and control the few employees who don't do the right thing and take advantage of their fellow employees and the company. Unfortunately, these policies have not reduced the numbers who take advantage. What it has done is limit the creativity, initiative and imaginations of the majority of employees.

To reverse the years of damage done to the culture from all these policies requires an all-in commitment by management to change them. Employees want to be and feel trusted. CEOs and senior management must align around and make decisions based on the belief that employees can be trusted. When you do so, great things can—and will—happen.

Here are some specific actions we took at Abrasive Technology (www.abrasive-tech.com) that led to meaningful, long-term change and truly transformed our organization. You can do it too! We can guide you through these 13 steps to simplify and transform your culture, leadership team and organizational structure.

Here are some results you can expect:

Key Business Metrics

- Increase Profitability
- Increase Productivity
- Improve Quality
- Improve Delivery
- Reduce Customer Complaints
- Reduce Voluntary Turnover

Cultural Improvements

- Employees more involved in daily decision-making
- Greater engagement, collaboration and accountability
- More flexible, agile and innovative environment
- More smiles & a strong sense of community
- Millennial-friendly environment

Start now by reading our book,
Manufacturing with Heart: A Holistic Approach
or give us a call…let's talk!
614-571-8586

13. Abandon recognition programs

Instead of recognition programs, build a culture of recognition.

What

Recognitions programs are bureaucratic and formal. They require scheduled, public recognitions of individual achievements.

A culture of recognition celebrates individual or group accomplishments as they occur with genuine appreciation.

Why

Most people want to be sincerely appreciated for what they do. Recognition programs lack sincerity. They are an obligation and one more administrative task to be completed. Genuine feeling is usually missing.

Recognition programs are often put in place in response to poor showings in employee surveys. They motivate people only for what's on the reward list. Rewards are transactional. "Programs" are always great in the beginning, but fade after a few weeks or months. When programs become the reason to be involved and the games fade, so does the involvement.

Building a culture where recognition and acknowledgment of individuals' work, performance, successes and contribution are a part of what everyone does every day is a more effective, long-term way of building employee involvement and motivation. Genuine, personal, specific and spontaneous appreciation can have a transformational effect on the culture, creating greater collaboration, trust, and well-being.

How

1. Listen. Actively listen. There is nothing people want more than to feel they have been heard.
2. Give the people around you feedback and often. Research concludes you need to give 10 positive feedbacks to every 1 negative or "constructive" feedback. So look and listen harder to catch people doing good stuff as much as letting them know about a problem or something they need to improve.
3. During Annual and Quarterly Meetings – Publicly recognize significant achievements by employees and/or teams.
4. Show Appreciation for individuals, teams and all employees with celebrations often and consistently. Do not go overboard or lavish. Keep things simple. Throw a pizza party for a good quarter or bring in a taco truck to thank production for getting a major customer's order out on time. Always recognize why you are celebrating.

5. Encourage managers to talk about good things happening. How do they relate to goals or values in company?
6. Annual appreciation dinners or luncheons can be a group celebration of dependability, loyalty and sharing stories of successes and failures during the year.

Obstacles

1. Management's desire for "programs" because they are defined and easy.
2. Developing leaders to be sincerely interested in the well-being of their team members.
3. Management too focused on solving problems. Encourage yourself and others to focus as much or more on the strengths of individuals, departments and the company than problems or weaknesses.

Results

1. Real and long-term involvement and motivation
2. Employees come to understand and appreciate that their involvement and innovation are a part of their jobs and therefore, the ongoing success of the company
3. Creates a more Positive and Productive Workplace

12. Stop hiring for skills only

Don't focus on skills, focus on culture.

What

Traditional companies have limited themselves by hiring and promoting people based solely on skill sets. Exceptional skill levels often led to "supervisor" or "manager" position as a reward for that skill.

By focusing on culture, the whole company benefits. An optimistic community provides the basic environment to encourage employees to work together to get the work done in the most efficient and collaborative ways.

Why

Exceptional performance in a position was rewarded by promotions to higher-level jobs that individuals may have been poorly suited to, often without necessary cultural support for learning.

Every company has a culture, whether it's been designed and developed, or it just happened. Problems occur when cultural awareness and support are missing. When management is only interested in hard metrics, it can easily turn a blind eye to workplace bullying. In such a culture people try to protect themselves, their jobs, and bargain for salary and benefits by hoarding knowledge. This sort of organization has a learning disability.

Culture matters. With a focus on task metrics, the culture element of the work place has been an underutilized resource for profitability. Task skills are easier to teach than people development. Culture is the collective attitudes and behaviors of people within a company. By developing an atmosphere of trust with shared learning, cross-training, and support as norms, companies respond to rapid change, lower workforce stress, and create a more congenial workplace.

How

There must be the belief and understanding that culture trumps all other attributes of individual and company performance. The performance of the entire organization by multiple measures of performance will be enhanced if those that diminish the positive culture are either coached to be a productive part of the team or let go.

1. Assess Current Workforce

   Determine where each employee is relative to task skills and company culture. A simple way to make this determination is to plot task skill (performance of the work) versus culture (behavior & attitude) on a chart like the one below.

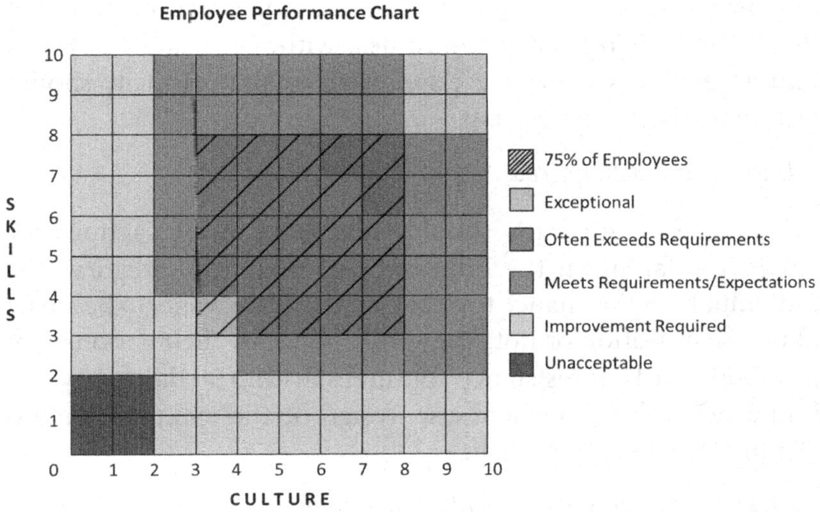

To make the skill/culture determination, arrange a meeting of each department's foreman, supervisor, or manager along with a representative from the human resources department. Review each employee, by department, for their skill and culture on a scale from 1-10 (1 being low and 10 being excellent). Have the group agree on a rating for each category and plot it onto the chart.

Repeat this process for each department and then assemble the information for the entire company into one chart. The company chart will indicate which employees need further development to improve their task skills and/or attitudes and behaviors.

2. Actions for Current Workforce

Unacceptable *Final Written Warning*

Managers and HR should take immediate action for employees falling in the Unacceptable category. The individual has the chance to decide whether he wants to be a part of the organization or not. They will choose by their actions, not just their words. If resistance continues, within 30 days, they will find a new job somewhere else, resign or the company should terminate their employment.

Improvement Required	*Verbal Warning*

Managers and HR should take immediate action for employees falling in the Improvement Required category. The individual has the chance to decide whether he wants to be a part of the organization or not. They will choose by their actions, not just their words. If resistance continues, within 90 days, they will find a new job somewhere else, resign or the company should terminate their employment

Meets Requirements/Expectations	*Support / Positive Feedback*
Often Exceeds Requirements	*Support / Positive Feedback*
Exceptional	*Encourage them to help others*

3. Redefine Hiring Process

With the understanding of the skills and culture within the organization, the hiring process will also need to change. The emphasis should be on the intelligence and attitude that a new hire would bring to support the core values of the organization. There may be a need for heavy skill orientation in some positions, such as machinists or accounts, while many of the task skills required for jobs within a company will need to be trained. Better to start with the cultural fit and then bring the skills up to speed.

Obstacles

1. Management will offer many "logical" reasons why the change cannot happen now, the end of the month, a big order in house or vacations scheduled, but the real reasons will include the following:

a. Difficult for them to fire anyone
b. Fear losing "irreplaceable" skills
c. Fear they can't find or train someone to do same level of task performance
d. May lose a bonus as productivity will go down in the short term
e. Fear of change in general

2. Managers do not like to change the current conditions or employees out of fear about what will happen. Even if today it is not good, the fear of things being worse is always present and colors the view of the positive that could be. Where someone has a skill or productivity that is good, unique and needed, it is difficult to want to fire the individual, especially, for the less measureable affect that their actions are having on the team by being disruptive or a non-team player. With the knowledge that a positive culture can be productive and by reducing the fear of the future, a manager can make the right choices for the long-term benefit of the organization.

Results

1. Productivity and shipments will fall for a short period of time while the team adjusts to the new environment and needs of the business. Employees will soon notice the change in atmosphere and begin to collaborate. Management needs to start to work with the teams while they are adjusting to the change and offer them the opportunity to be involved in improving the departments' operations. How do we fill the skill and make improvements for the customer experience?
2. Employees will have more faith in management when a low culture employee is separated. Employees are looking at management to take action on disruptive employees and

saying "why is this person here?" Changing out employees who have an extremely low culture score is the fastest way to change the culture and make a statement about the direction of the company and the importance of culture. These individuals are doing more harm to the organization than you can ever imagine or believe.

3. As others see that management is serious about the culture of the organization, employees will begin to believe that the culture is changing. Management can increase the education on core values, expectations and norms for the company and customer. As more employees accept and act within these norms, a tipping point will occur that will create momentum for further improvement.
4. Management spends more time with the 80% of involved employees, not the 20% causing problems.
5. Management just doesn't have the constant trivial complaints that they spend so much time on every day. Problems and conflicts are resolved between the employees and disagreement on direction or actions can be discussed with a third party to make a decision.

11. It's the way you say it

Eliminate culture-damaging language; opt for culture-building language.

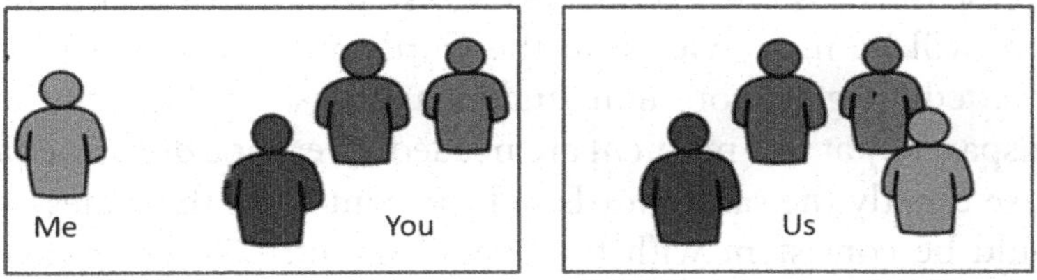

What

Word choice is a function of culture. Culture damaging language describes what happens when the words we use are unwittingly toxic.

Awareness of how words impact people is the foundation of culture building language.

Why

Language conveys emotional meaning. The words you use can build or destroy culture. For example, "you people" disconnects the "superior" speaker from listeners. This phrase creates divisions.

Collaborative, inclusive language allows people to communicate in positive ways compatible with the direction of company goals—our equipment rather than my machine, my desk or my computer. Our team rather than my team. Simply paying attention to pronouns makes a big difference to people!

How

It is critical for everyone to use a common language to develop a culture of trust and collaboration between employees and within the company. Common language, definitions and understanding do not happen in a vacuum. Management needs to spend time discussing the language and how their actions can increase the possibility of success within the entire organization. There will be many views on the words and actions. All must be vetted to gain common understandings. Authenticity and transparency at this moment are needed. Everyone does not have to use exactly the same words but the context of their messages should be consistent with the overall intent. Like positive and negative feedback, it takes 10 positive language statements to gain back ground lost by one negative language error.

1. Glossary of Words & Their Meanings

Include technical, processes and financial terms, team names, mantras and acronyms. This can be very useful for new employees to help them more quickly feel a part of the company and less like an outsider when they are talking with others.

Defining mantras is a good way to maintain the involvement of people. An important one is DWYSYWD, or Do What You Say You Will Do. This simple mantra becomes a way of operating, generates trust and collaboration. No one has to worry about what is going to get done and when. For example, after a team has assigned tasks to individuals or a project deadline has been agreed or a goal set, no one needs to follow up. The person does not feel managed or continually asked how they are doing. If they have a problem doing what they agreed, they will ask for help or tell other stakeholders what is happening.

2. Employee to Associate

The word employee sounds servile and detached. Change from using the word employee to "associate" or use your own term. Then define the characteristics of an associate as shown in the example below. Help people feel part of a productive group, passionate about getting work done and sharing in the rewards.

Definition of an Associate

Members of the team, committed and loyal to the organization and its employees, who enthusiastically believe in a win-win and lose-lose partnership, take pride in their daily tasks, show respect for themselves and others, and are accountable for their actions.

Associate	Employee
Accountable / Responsible	Entitled
Collaborate	Isolate
Conscientious	Indifferent
Customer-driven (internal and external)	Works for a paycheck
Dependable	Inconsistent
Desire	Required
Engaged	Disconnected
Works in team environment	Works alone
Flexible	Resists change
Flow	Push or pull through
Initiative	Tell me what to do
Innovative	Complacent
Interdependent	Dependent
Learns from mistakes	Fears consequences of mistakes
Likes to learn	Teach me, train me, tell me
Makes decisions	Needs approval from others
Motivated	"8 and hit the gate"

Associate	**Employee (cont.)**
Positive contributor	Going through the motions
Risk taker	Afraid to make mistakes
Sharing	Territorial
Team success	Self-success
Trusting, Trustworthy	Skeptical, Untrustworthy
We	I / Me

3. Manager to Leader

Leaders need to come from a leadership perspective to want the best for the corporation and its Associates. Below is an example comparing Leader versus Manager for more clarity of the actions and feelings that will generate a win-win approach.

Manage vs.	**Lead**
Manager	Leader
Direct	Engage
Control	Influence
Listen	Question/Listen
Instruct	Learn
Dominate	Motivate
Separate	Integrate
I'm Right	Multiple Rights
Argue	Dialogue
Command	Invite
Mine	Ours

4. Attention to Pronouns

Developing a more collaborative environment cannot be done without the use of a language that is compatible with this effort. It is very easy to destroy months of collaborative, culture building work by using the wrong pronoun at the wrong time. Use inclusive words such as we, us and ours. We all have equipment or desks that we use every day. How do you refer to them when talking? This is MY desk or MY computer or MY lathe. Does that mean that others cannot use the equipment? Is it really YOURS or is it owned by the company and you are using it.

Obstacles

1. People have used divisive language and "my" pronouns for a very long time. With the Industrial Revolution, we had the growth of unions, which made a big distinction between labor and management. Even where unions existed, corporations generated their own distinction through a hierarchy of titles, location, perks and attitude.
2. Many managers hold on to the command and control way of thinking and acting.
3. Individuals, whether manager or labor, and often do not believe in their heart and gut that building trust and collaboration is a good approach to business viability. These individuals, with effort and thinking very hard, can usually say the right words but there is often a look, a nod or an added word that shows I don't believe what I just said. These are passive resistive people who will not help the organization and need to be coached in or out.

Results

1. Culture will change as the common understanding of the language and actions become more universal.
2. The real start of collaboration. Employees will be more helpful and forthcoming with information needed to make a quality product. Less scrap due to better communication.
3. Better understanding of Direction, Alignment and Commitment.

10. Not just for those at the top

Turn leadership development into employee development.

What

Leadership development is the norm for management.

Employee development expands leadership development to everyone in the company and transforms employees into a community of leaders.

Why

Manufacturers spend millions of dollars on leadership training for managers to improve productivity and profitability, while the largest expense and greatest potential for improvement goes wanting, your employees.

Your company benefits when all the people within it function at higher levels. When people have greater self-awareness, they become better listeners and so communicate more skillfully with their peers.

Employees can take on more responsibility and learn a wider range of tasks through development. As people learn greater respect for others and recognize their own dignity, teams function more effectively. Development leads to greater awareness of the needs of individuals and common corporate goals.

How

1. Define the organization's strategy for vertical and horizontal development.

Horizontal development includes all the training for hard task skills—from machining and assembly to accounting and information technologies. Learning and improving on how to do what we do is critical for all businesses.

Vertical development includes assessments for self-awareness—Myers Briggs Type Indicator (MBTI), FIRO-B, EQ, and Change Indicator are examples. These programs offer deep self-awareness and if done with teams, offer deeper awareness not only of the self but of team members which provides greater opportunity for alignment and commitment to groups, projects or goals.

2. Team building

Many team development or teambuilding exercises are available for free on the Internet. Most of them work because 80% of the effectiveness is simply due to time spent being together working on gaining a better understanding the dynamics of working in teams, more personal relationship development and communications skills.

3. Framing

The Chapter titled, "It's the Way You Say It: Culture-Damaging Language to Culture-Building Language", talks about how important language can be to change the culture of the organization. How much different does it sound to say that we have an Employee Development Plan versus a Leadership Development Plan. This reframing puts everyone on a more even playing field to bring the entire corporation up to a different level.

Obstacles

1. Employees just want to do their tasks. There may be some complaining about taking time from production for the soft skills training. This often comes from employees who what to come to work every day, but be left alone at their machine or their place in assembly, not talk with anyone and make "their parts".
2. Some managers are afraid of losing their authority.
3. Some people fear being open about themselves.

Results

The right combination of horizontal and vertical development for all employees changes everything:

- Improved task skills will provide less scrap, better quality and lower costs.
- Improved self-awareness will provide better behaviors and better attitudes which will encourage employees to make more decisions and move to the work to reduce bottlenecks and improve production flow, which will reduce late shipments and delivery times.
- Better decisions throughout organization—all levels
- Greater awareness of and compassion for self and others
- More effective communications
- Resistance changes to appreciation

9. Trust in transparency

End arbitrary pay; choose compensation plans.

What

Pay is arbitrary and secret.

Openly share compensation plans which match pay within nationally published pay ranges.

Why

Rumors grow in the dark. When pay is secret, employees imagine other people and departments are being better compensated than they are. Secrecy breeds dissent and dissatisfaction.

People are more concerned about fairness of their pay. Demonstrating the relationship of skills and pay for the region shows people their pay is consistent with those with similar skills. Transparency fosters trust.

How

1. Establish a Compensation Review Team to create a simple and clear Compensation Program. Be honest, open and publish the information. Make your philosophy and strategy clear with the ultimate goal of removing the dissatisfaction around wages.
2. Find national, regional and local compensate data surveys. Determine where your wages fall relative to the survey data. Make changes to wages to coincide with your compensation philosophy and strategy.
3. Once your pay and pay ranges are aligned with the data surveys, publish them both so employees can see they are being paid fairly for their work. Let people know what your philosophy, strategies, wages, benefits and bonuses are relative to the data surveys.
4. Provide fast, consistent, open and honest responses to questions about pay.
5. Put an end to the Performance Review Process which no one likes or trusts and start across-the-board annual increases. Adjust individual pay when significant changes in responsibilities occur. Use Individual Development Programs for growth and learning and/or performance problems when they happen, rather than waiting for annual performance reviews. See Chapter 4: Say Goodbye to Employee Reviews for more details.
6. Be specific about pay (including base pays and bonuses), pay ranges, pay increases, benefits and their costs to the employee and the costs to the company. Make this information available for new hires and update changes with employees as they occur.

Obstacles

1. The wage compensation analysis may not present wage increases for everyone.

2. Being able to present the information in a way that people can truly understand all of the dynamics surrounding pay.
3. When employees review the compensation data and job descriptions they are likely to argue that their tasks or more in line with a job paying more.
4. Employees will complain about across-the-board annual increases.

Results

1. Takes the constant complaining about the fairness of pay off the table
2. Eliminates time-consuming system of performance appraisals
3. The transparency creates trust
4. Employees believe they are paid appropriately

8. Throw away what you don't need

Move from employee policies to an employee guidebook.

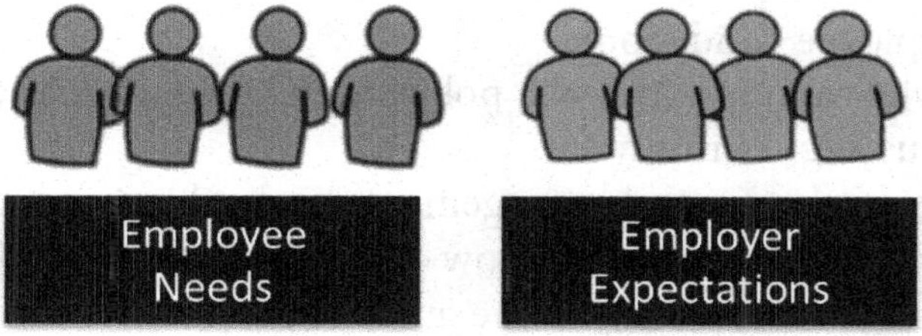

What

An employee policy manual contains legal requirements, rules, and alienating restrictions.

An employee guidebook communicates the company's goals and expectations. While retaining legal requirements, makes people feel a part of the company and advises them on what they can do, rather than what they can't do.

Why

Policies are necessary, but they limit action. Employee policy manuals are cumbersome, take time to maintain, and waste administrative effort. Except for those legally required, many policies are without value. Moreover, language in employee policy handbooks is harsh, demanding, and alienating. Without trust there can only be rules and surveillance.

An employee guidebook gives employees an understanding of the background of the company, and their place in it. By use of friendly, functional, and inclusive language, a guidebook communicates how the company is structured, what the company is doing for the employee, and what the company expects in return. Legal requirements are inserted at the end of the book. Trust frees resources.

How

1. HR leads a project to transform a Policy Manual into an Employee Guidebook.
2. Review and modify each policy with language that creates a trusting environment.
3. Get employees and management involved in the process. Ask what they want to know or get more clarity about. Ask them to review parts of the guidebook that may be relevant to them and request feedback, then incorporate their ideas and suggestions.
4. Change the tone of the Guidebook from one of dos and don'ts to one of support and encouragement.
5. Include all the legally required policies at the end of the guidebook.

Obstacles

1. Management need for specific command and control rules and regulations.
2. Belief that legal requirements go farther than they really do.

Results

1. Creates a more trusting environment.
2. Improves collaboration and collective creativity.
3. Reduces many hours of unnecessary work for data collection and reconciliation.

7. Put your oxygen mask on first

Integrate the needs of the customer with the welfare of the company, employees and other stakeholders.

What

The customer is number one and always right. Business is there to only serve customer needs.

Integrate the needs of customer, company, employees, and other stakeholders.

Why

"The customer is always right" is a slogan from London's Selfridges Department Store in an early 20th-century publicity campaign. The idea stuck. But in its extreme form it hurts everyone, and ultimately the customer when unprofitable negotiations lead to supplier bankruptcy. If customers are always right, they can buy at whatever price, delivery and payment terms they choose and behave badly.

Every company is focused on helping customers. Decision making, such as whether to take on new projects, should be made with respect to capabilities, work-in-progress, and the needs of other stakeholders. Suppliers must beware of customers' demands for pricing, delivery, and payment terms that are unprofitable, cause delays, or interfere with current projects.

How

1. Management commitment

The concept of integration needs to be established by management and perpetuated throughout the organization as the way to do business for the long term. It is the best long term approach to be transparent with customers. Doing the right thing will win in the long run! Customer being #1 may be a good slogan but can, when taken to it illogical conclusion, put any company out of business.

2. Training is Key

Employees who have direct contact with customers, including Management, customer service and sales, need to have the same training as the customers' purchasing agents. These buyers have been trained in how to negotiate and use the strength of their "order" to win concessions. An important element of any negotiation is that, as a supplier, you have more power than you think. Look at the power of saying no. It is used to let the buyer know that what is being asked is beyond what the company is willing to do.

Employees in production and the support processes should be trained to understand the importance of integrating the needs of customers, employees and the company in their decision making.

3. Limits

Employees need grounded in the limits of their authority to make company decisions without the need to talk with others for their perspectives. To negotiate well, employees need to be extremely familiar with the operation and the limitations that are imposed by the production system. Everyone in the company will do everything possible to meet the commitment to the customer.

4. Management support of employee actions.

Reversing employee decisions will undermine their authority and stop them from making future decisions. If bad decisions are made, allow the employee to correct the decisions rather than management reversing them directly with the customer.

Obstacles

1. When there is a lot of stress within the organization for delivery or low order input, customer service, engineering and/or the quotation person could go back to the old model of doing whatever the customer wants to get an order. They may take business that would be unprofitable or only short-term business.
2. Customers do not want to hear about the company issues with meeting their expressed need. The purchasing agent's job is to get the supplies needed at the terms that they want. This becomes more difficult to generate balance when the products that a company produces are a pure commodity.
3. The company could lose an order because they could not meet their terms or other issues.
4. Managers want to help by answering directly to customers but may undermine previous decisions.

Results

1. Generates a powerful message to all employees that the company is in business for the long term, has integrity and is interested in more than money and orders. Without it there is the feeling that the company is being taken advantage of which does not feel right to the employees who do feel a part of the company.
2. Reduces the need for expedites.
3. Increases profitability due to better terms and improved productivity.
4. Produces a positive dialogue with the customer to foster a solid, long-term relationship built on realistic expectations and knowledge of the capabilities.

6. Stop playing the budget game

Retire top-down budgeting; teach collaborative budgeting.

What

There are two players in the top-down budgeting game: executives and middle managers. Executives demand unrealistic budget tightening. Middle managers pad their needs to compensate.

Collaborative budgeting seeks input from everyone. Each process team submits their priorities. Budgets are project and outcome driven.

Why

Each party in the top-down budgeting game knows the other is often lying. Now time-wasting negotiations commence. Executives make across-the-board percentage cuts reducing everyone's ability to function at an optimal level.

Collaborative budgeting is a result of input from everyone. All employees have practical suggestions for projects and what they need to do their jobs for the coming year. Process groups decide on their priorities among themselves. Instead of across-the-board cuts, some projects are abandoned, leaving those which are selected to be fully funded.

Employees gain understanding about the financial side of business through discussions with their teams in prioritizing their wants and needs for the budget.

Gain direction, alignment and commitment (DAC) of the entire organization.

How

1. Limit the number of customers, products, projects or actions to those that will make a real difference in the overall profitability of the company.
2. All input is based on the best estimates and not from a point of negotiation.
3. Bonus system is not based on the budget which avoids building conflict into the process.
4. Business Roadmap Process Outline:

Determine Direction

Business Strategy Meeting

1. Short-Term Direction
2. Long-Term Vision

All Departments Team Meetings

1. Ideas for Process Improvements
2. What does it take: People, Projects & Capital Expenditures?
3. Expected results—What is the expected return for company and customers?

Gain Alignment

Global Leadership Meeting

1. Global Economic Forecast Review
2. Present and discuss results from Process Team Meetings
3. Time to connect and collaborate

Business Strategy Meeting

From a company-wide, global and long-term perspective, evaluate the financial impact of the input from the roadmap process, ensure alignment with long-term vision and agree on the extent to which the company can fund the requested:

1. Capital Expenditures & Significant Discretionary Spending
2. Proposed Goals
3. Proposed Projects
4. Manpower Additions

Gain Commitment

Business Strategy & Leadership Team Meeting

- Discuss and agree upon the final Roadmap

January Kick-Off Meetings (All Employee)

- Present Roadmap Summary

Managers review with their teams the final goals and specific projects for their group.

Final Business Roadmap Includes:

1. Assumptions
2. Economic Perspective
3. Focus, Products & Markets
4. Capital Expenditures, Projects & Discretionary Spending
5. Manpower required

6. Financials by Process
7. Cash Forecast
8. Goals by Process

Obstacles

1. Not having relationships of trust and collaboration within the management team.
2. Resistance by managers for having to spend the time working with employees to get them involved, understand the importance of planning and gaining their input.
3. Managers want to spend time on:
   -Detail costs of each program and expense
   -Fancy presentations
   -Quantity of projects included in presentations rather than the most important projects that would make a difference in productivity, quality, delivery or profitability.
   -5-10% improvements rather than the more difficult 25-50% improvement projects
4. Over committing on what can be done.

Results

1. Employee involvement. Employees learn about the difficulties and realities of budgeting, the same as individuals have to do with their finances. Sometimes there is a belief that there are unlimited funds since it is a corporation.
2. A more realistic roadmap.
3. A few important projects and goals that will move the corporation forward.
4. Clear Direction, Alignment and Commitment from and for the entire organization.
5. No time spent on constant Roadmap revisions because the Collaborative Business Roadmap is a roadmap and not a document to measure performance or determine pay.

The Roadmap P&L is not recalculated once completed. The purpose of the work is to gain DAC which is done. It is a fluid document for manpower, capital, projects and discretionary expenses as the needs unfold throughout the year.

5. Be here now

Let go of attendance policies; create attendance guidelines.

What

Attendance policies specify mandatory rules for being at work, and under what conditions employees can work overtime, take sick time, personal days, and vacation.

Attendance guidelines communicate the needs of the company, what's expected from employees, and how to talk about their individual needs with their teams and managers.

Why

Over the last 100 years, companies have progressively added more restrictions. Policing attendance takes time and leads to an absurdity: tracking the time it takes to track time. Managers were required to make judgments about whether the excuses for time off were valid.

Attendance policy manuals can run to 50 pages or more of things employees can't do.

Simplify a long list of unnecessary restrictions with a short list of expectations.

In a culture of trust you can get rid of attendance policy, free up administrative time, remove the need for judgments about time off, make people feel more responsible and respected. Trust generates loyalty and dedication.

How

Following is a template for a simple attendance guideline which can be used with your modifications and inserted into your own employee handbook.

Attendance Guideline

Regular attendance and punctuality are very important to the success of the company--they go a long way to ensure that we can efficiently meet our internal and external customers' needs for product quality, consistency and delivery. There are times employees cannot make regularly scheduled work hours and/or be at work due to illness or family situations. Chronic (or routine) absenteeism and/or tardiness within any process is extremely disruptive to process flow and customer deliveries. Attendance is a part of employee dependability and may reduce or eliminate merit increases. Time off work will be monitored by and discussed with Coaches. If a process team's performance is suffering due to an Employee's poor attendance or punctuality, the following process should be followed:

1. Process team members: discuss the problem in a meeting with all team members present to determine if there is a way to change the problem. Discuss possible changes to

Employee's schedule that would be acceptable to all team members and still ensure work completion. If this fails,

2. Process team members: consult with Coach. Our Company philosophy on attendance is a positive one: we will attempt to coach any Employee to become a dependable team member. If team meetings and/or coaching fail to resolve the problem, there may be disciplinary actions necessary, up to and including separation.

Work Hours

- The Company's customer business hours are Monday through Friday, 8am to 5pm EST.
- Each process/shift has designated work hours, which are listed on the attached worksheet and posted on the process intranet site.
- Each Employee has scheduled work hours, which are listed within her/his Process sheet on the intranet site.
- All Employees are encouraged to take a lunch break. Times allotted per process are listed on the attached worksheet.

Attendance Guideline

- Be at work, on time, for scheduled work hours
- Hourly Employees
  - o Log in when working and log out when not working
- Salary Employees
  - o Record all time/hours worked and record time/hours not worked during scheduled work hours
- Schedule time off with team members, including manager whenever possible; register scheduled time off with Administrative Support Team (ASPT) Member; ASPT will enter info into on-line company calendar for easy access
- For unscheduled time off, phone into Attendance Hotline (see instructions below) -- ASPT members will ensure

your team (and others as designated) are notified of your absence

Vacation, Sick & Personal (VSP) Time Off

- Is relative to years of service in current year

Years of Service	*Vacation Days*	*Sick/Personal Days*
Less than 5 years	#	#
5 to 10 years	#	#
Over 10 years	#	#

- Is available for new employees after the 90th day of employment
  - o Any time missed during the initial 90 days of employment will be unpaid
- Is shown on the paycheck stub each pay period
- Vacation time which is unused at the end of the calendar year, up to a maximum of 40 hours, will carry over into the next calendar year.
- Part-time employee Time Off will be calculated separately based on scheduled hours per year
- Any employee with unscheduled absence from work and does not call the attendance recorder for three consecutive days will be considered a three-day no call/no show. We will accept this as immediate voluntary resignation
- If an employee provides at least a one-week notice and has worked a minimum of 90 days, he/she will be paid for all earned and unused vacation time on the final paycheck. However, no payment for vacation time will be made if the employee fails to give proper notice of his/her resignation. Employees who are separated by the Company will be paid out any earned and unused vacation time.

Scheduling Time Off

- Each process team should post a time off calendar in their process work area
- Requests for time off should be submitted to Employee's Team (including Manager)
- Requests for time off should be submitted as long before needed as possible to help team members plan for the absence
- Team agreement to requests for time off should be based on work volume and staffing needs of the process and coverage available. If there is a conflict or disagreement among the team members for a time off request, the team's manager or a member of the HR team will make a decision and/or settle any conflict after consulting with the manager for effects on Quality, Delivery and Costs
- Employees are responsible to call the attendance hotline (see call in instructions below) for scheduled time off and on each day of unscheduled absence.

Attendance Hotline

When an employee is going to be absent from work or arrive later than the scheduled start time (whether scheduled or unscheduled) the employee is responsible to call the attendance hotline unless physically unable to do so. Except for Designated Time Off or scheduled time off, employees are expected to call the attendance recorder each day of the absence before their scheduled start time. Employees calling into the attendance recorder should clearly state:

- First and Last Name
- Department
- Time or day expected to return to work

The Attendance Hotline is 1-800-XXX-XXX, Dial XXX to Access Voice Mail System.

COMPANY DESIGNATED TIME OFF:

Holidays & Plant Shutdown

Employees will be paid for Company designated holidays and plant shutdown as posted annually on our Intranet site. Employees who have an unscheduled absence the day before or after a Company designated holiday or plant shutdown will be paid for the time off if Vacation, Sick or Personal Time is available.

Voluntary Time Off (VTO)

If work volume is low, a manager may, at their discretion, offer VTO to employees. If an employee takes VTO when offered he/she could choose to use VSP or unpaid time.

Bereavement

Employees may take up to three consecutive work days off with pay following the death of the employee's current legal spouse, parent, child, step child, step parent, brother, sister, grandparent, grandparents-in-law, brother-in-law, sister-in-law, legal guardian, grandchild, mother-in-law, father-in-law, son-in-law, or daughter-in-law.

Extended Leave of Absence

Employees with at least one-year of service may request an unpaid, extended leave of absence. A formal request for leave should be made to employee's manager and will be granted based on business needs. Employees on extended leave of absence are required to continue their bi-weekly benefit (medical, dental, etc.) contributions. Any extended leave of absences granted will not necessarily guarantee a job upon return to work.

Weather Emergency

If weather conditions cause any facility to close, the attendance hotline will have a recording stating the facility will be closed.

Jury Summons

We encourage employees to serve on jury duty when called. Employees should notify their Team Members and Human Resources of the need for time off for jury duty as soon as a notice of summons from the court or a subpoena is received. A copy of the jury duty summons or subpoena must be submitted to Human Resources or Administrative Support Team Member prior to the requested service date. Jury leave is paid for up to a maximum of two weeks in a calendar year.

Medical Leave (FMLA) or Military Leave

See separate policies for detailed information and requirements.

EMPLOYEE ATTENDANCE AND TIME OFF GUIDELINES

This guideline applies to regular status employees. Temporary employees are not eligible.

Process/Shift Designated Work Hours:

Process	***Work Hours***	***Lunch***
Customer Service	8 to 5	1 HOUR
Human Resources	8 to 5	1 HOUR w 24/7 coverage
IT	8 to 5	1 HOUR w 24/7 coverage
Marketing	8 to 5	1 HOUR
Production	7 to 3:30	1/2 HOUR
Leadership	8 to 5	1 HOUR

Obstacles

1. There will be skepticism among some employees. Consistent communications about the new guideline will help. It can take a while for employees to understand you are sincerely trying to show your trust in them and their work. They can find it hard to believe they are being given so much freedom to tell the truth and know they are being trusted.
2. Some employees will abuse the new system. For those few who do, show little tolerance for them. They often decide themselves to go elsewhere on their own. Your insistence on balancing the needs of the individual, the company and your customers through effective management of abusers will go a long way toward creating even more trust with the majority of people who do not abuse the new system.

Results

1. Less managerial time required to track each employee's time.
2. People can be honest and do not have to come up with excuses or lie to take a day off.
3. Trust is generated and received.
4. The process of generating the Attendance Guideline will help managers frame future decisions and actions. Be more flexible with people knowing that the company is in this direction. Think more about the 80%.

4. Say goodbye to employee reviews

Replace employee reviews with individual development plans.

What

Employee reviews look backward. They are judgments; assessments of past performance.

Individual employee development plans look forward. Their purpose is to fulfill company needs and help employees realize their future potential in both hard and soft skills.

Why

Only looking backward does little to prepare for an ever-changing environment. There is value to looking at past performance, but it shouldn't stop there. What's missing with performance reviews is preparation and support for learning what hasn't yet been mastered.

Employee development plans are designed for individuals and aligned with company, process and individual goals. Development plans offer continual support to help employees learn rather than only judge past performance.

The Individual Employee Development Plan (IEDP) process is intended to align the capabilities of employees and their commitment to the direction of a company's long-term business strategies, culture and annual goals by:

- Facilitating the engagement, development and learning of employees;
- Focusing on continuous improvement through individual development, learning and moving to the work (See Chapter 2 – Jump Around);
- Acknowledging and honoring every employee's individuality, and unique skills and talents;
- Targeting gaps in task skills and behaviors;
- Employing collaborative efforts between employees and management;
- Creating action plans for individuals to become more engaged in their own success and growth;
- Coaching for performance and accountability.

How

1. Define an overall strategy and reasons for the change from Performance Reviews to the IEDP for the Company. Then develop a process for the IEDP's as the replacement for Performance Reviews. Share the strategy and process outline with all employees, preferably in a meeting that includes everyone at the same time.
2. Managers meet with team members to clearly define their department's Mission, Objectives, Capabilities, Process Tasks, Expectations and Behaviors so everyone has a shared understanding of their responsibilities. This assumes the above categories exist for the company as a whole. If not, those should be clarified by the owner, President, a member of the HR team and top management as a template for each department to use. Simplify as much as possible for clarity.

3. By department, create a worksheet or database of the mission, objectives, capability, tasks, expectations and behaviors for tracking with levels of proficiency required to do the work. Managers should rank each employee according to their perception and employees should rank themselves. Then they should meet and come to a shared understanding before moving forward.
4. Once the beginning rankings are complete for all employees in the department, managers should develop a matrix of knowledge and capability levels for each associate within a department, determine the gaps, and plan for gap closure. Managers should meet with employees as needed (minimum once/quarter) to define and document goals to fill gaps in performance or behaviors. It is very important that the goals be SMART (specific, measurable, attainable, realistic and timely).

INDIVIDUAL EMPLOYEE DEVELOPMENT PLAN

Associate Name: ______________________

Goal: ______________________

Date Discussed: ______________________

Measurable Action Steps: ______________________

Date To Be Completed: ______________________

Reason for Goal/Benefit: ______________________

Review, Insights, Comments, Learning: ______________________

5. If an employee meets or exceeds skills, expectations and behavior, managers should also offer possibilities for other more long-term developmental goals; are there other areas in the company that the employee would like to investigate; perhaps offer a mentoring or part time apprentice program for another job? Are there special projects the employee could lead for the experience? Let the employee know you are interested in them for the long-term; that you want to help them meet their personal work goals as well as those of the company and department.
6. For all employees, encourage commitment to goal achievement, discuss reasons for incomplete goal achievement, and take any actions that may be required, up to and including dismissal. Document and share the documentation of all conversations with the employee to ensure shared understanding between management and employee.
7. Employees will be responsible to work with managers to develop the Individual Employee Development Plan, commit to achieving the goals of the IEDP and provide progress reports for self-accountability and to manager (minimum once/quarter).

Obstacles

1. Fear of elimination of annual performance reviews that can be used for disciplinary actions
2. The initial implementation is time consuming
3. Concerns about fair pay

Results

1. Continuous improvement through individual development, learning and moving to the work
2. ISO Compliance with traceable documentation for training and learning

3. Spend less time on past performance, more focus on present and future development
4. More efficient processes – simplification
5. More trust is created with focused efforts on the strengths of employees by removing the performance appraisal/merit increase process that everyone basically labels "a joke". Please see Chapter 9 titled "Trust in Transparency."
6. Gives managers a strategic view for training needs and future hiring.

3. Stop approving

Abandon manager approvals in favor of employee accountability.

What

Manager approvals are procedures for documenting requests, making judgments to approve or deny allocation of funds.

Employee accountability doesn't need manager approvals. Budgets are allocated to teams so they can make their own decisions.

Why

Manager approvals have many layers. They're cumbersome and subject to communication errors. Filling out paperwork, even if it's online, can be an unnecessary habit. Managers are forced to make judgments without a lot of knowledge about the request. People's requests for approvals are almost always approved by the manager or administrative staff.

In all corporations there is a limited amount of resources, a seemingly unlimited list of needed resources and a limited amount of trust for the employees who need to allocate those resources. Therefore, a massive and abused system of sign off signatures has been put into place to accommodate the rules, regulations and hoops to get those resources.

A weakness with manager-approved purchases is that they remove responsibility for employees to think about the cost of what they're requesting.

Employee accountability works on the basis of trust and competency. Abandoning the approval process frees time, gets needed materials faster and speeds production. When people are treated as adults they usually respond that way. This has a positive impact on the whole organization. Having autonomy with accountability in one area is more likely to help people act responsibly in other areas.

"Just go get what you need when you need it" is an expression of trust and effectiveness.

How

1. Initiate an employee involvement project called "$3,000 fund" that demonstrates, rather than teaches, how difficult it is to use limited resources wisely. Every person faces this allocation of limited resources daily with trying to manage all the things they would like to have and do with a finite paycheck. Give $3,000 to each department to be spent by their team with these guidelines:
   a. Each member of the group puts forward a list of needs to be bought with the $3,000.
   b. The lists are then combined and given back to all members
   c. Each member prioritizes the list to spend all the $3,000

d. The prioritized lists are then put together to determine what the teams believes are the top items to be purchased without spending over the $3,000
e. The team then discusses whether to spend money on several lower cost/prioritized items versus a more expensive higher prioritized item.

It is amazing how much is learned in this exercise. A real understanding of how difficult it is to choose between very good alternatives. Some may have to wait until a later date.

Also, see Chapter 6, "Stop Playing the Budget Game".

2. After employees have what they need, they can begin to think in terms of the company and its needs. Create a system of broad limits for spending authority. As an example: for small companies, $5,000 for anyone, $5,000 to $25,000 with some conversation with the team and above $25,000 needs approval. Can add zeros to these amounts based on the sales of the company or choose other levels but keep it simple. Rather than managing every purchase, manage the team performance on spending to their goals. Encourage risk taking to make improvements.
3. Purchase requests go directly to purchasing or entered directly into the computer system by the employee.

Obstacles

1. Managers feeling a lack of control or importance.
2. Managers fear expenses will increase by letting employees buy what they need.
3. Employees fear making decisions and concerned if they will be second guessed and make a mistake that will hurt their ability to keep their job, get a new job or get a raise.

Results

1. Removes the need to find someone to sign off on every request.
2. Requests for approvals will be significantly reduced
3. Reduces the time it takes to get what is needed.
4. Replaces the assessment of managers with the assessment of employees or their teams.
5. Enhances the culture of trust and involvement.
6. Employees get what they need to do their tasks.

2. Jump around

Stop focusing just on fixed tasks and move to the work.

What

Fixed tasks are mechanical operations. Traditionally, people were only trained for one job. They were required to complete simple and repetitive tasks with little understanding of the bigger process in which they worked.

Move to the work is more than being cross-trained. It is for individuals to understand the whole process and their place in it. They learn how bottlenecks occur and how to address them.

Why

Today repetitive, task-based skills are the domain of robots. Any failure in a task-based line will create bottlenecks resulting in breakdowns, decreased productivity, and delays.

Move to the work increases productivity. Move to the work expands employees' capabilities and awareness of the whole organization. They can look in front of them and behind and move to where they're needed without managers telling them where to go. Employees have more autonomy. By learning more and better skills, they increase value to themselves and the company. Move to the work demonstrates a company's agility making the company less vulnerable to weak links and therefore more resilient and robust.

How

There are two ways to prepare employees to move to the work. The first is straight-forward training/learning. The second is a more robust process redesign with training/learning that requires rethinking how the tasks should be assembled.

1. The easiest and fastest way is to train several employees for a series of tasks that are close in proximity or tasks that are done just before or just after the primary task. The tasks remain individual tasks and located where they have been but have several employees trained for them. Each employee will have a primary task where his current skill or experience is best utilized. This group of employees will have a series of tasks or operations that they are responsible to do. The employees will learn from the employee who has more experience in each task.
2. Managers teach how to collaborate on how best to move to the work to get the tasks completed. As employees become more capable, they can see if something has changed or a bottle neck has occurred within these tasks that may require they move from their primary task. The employees can now float between several tasks as they see appropriate to improve the part flow. The movement may be required due to not being able to fully balance the process times of the tasks, a quality problem or a change in efficiency.
3. After training several employees in several tasks in one process, the concept can be expanded to train tasks in more than one process. They could then move between

processes to eliminate a bottleneck caused by a lack of people or the efficiency of equipment resources.

4. A "job jar" or "open job list" is an effective way for employees to move to a task where they have been trained or which requires very little skill. Each day all department managers would provide tasks where help was needed for the day. So, an employee whose tasks were completed could go to the job jar to help elsewhere.

Obstacles

1. Some employees only want to do one job or don't have the skills to learn other tasks.
2. Quality can be a problem if the employee is not well trained on the task before moving to another task.
3. Some employees use this as a way to hide.
4. Pay levels may not be appropriate for the new task expertise.

Results

1. Production efficiencies as the person always has tasks to perform.
2. Less turnover because employees are happy that they do not have to do only one task all day long.
3. Improved flow of product throughout the process.
4. Innovation for process improvement as the employee is more involved.
5. Fewer inspection steps and better quality.
6. Eliminates hand offs and sitting time.

1. Get Flatter, Go Further

Change from traditional to a simpler, flatter, process-centered organization structure.

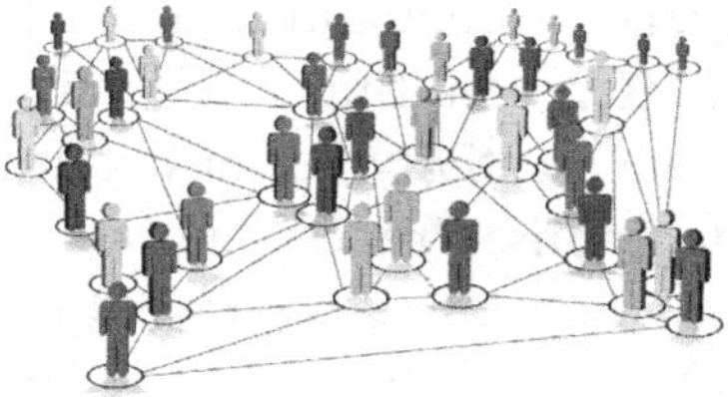

What

Traditional manufacturing companies are organized around product lines. Each product line has its own customer service, sales, management, etc., with a clear chain of command, many time-consuming rules, and managers who administer them. As long as conditions remain the same (which they never seem to do) traditional organizations can be efficient.

Process-centered organizations (PCOs) are aligned around processes, i.e., a collection of sequential tasks, such as finance, machining, or assembly. Teams are organized by process for all products. For example, finance teams work within the finance process. The PCO is a simpler, flatter, less costly organizational structure with process engineer and coach leaders rather than managers, creating a dual servant leadership model.

Why

Traditional structures are vulnerable to rapid change and increasingly become unattractive to 21st century workers. In its extreme form, the traditional hierarchy is authoritarian. When that happens people are afraid to offer suggestions for improvement. Innovation suffers when a company fails to engage the collective wisdom of its people. In the traditional structure each product line can be unaware of others, causing redundancies and inefficiencies.

By contrast, the PCO functions at a higher developmental level. Individuals learn more about and understand themselves and other people better, resulting in effective communication. PCO fosters collective creativity because it encourages teams to make their own decisions. Process engineers and coaches are responsible for removing barriers preventing employees from doing their jobs well. Environments of care and autonomy foster long-term loyalty, pride, and gratitude. Customers, the company, and employees win.

Here is the core belief of the process-centered organization concept:

If they are given the information and tools that they need to perform;
If they are provided with an understanding of customer requirements and of the big picture of the work;
If they are guided by clear measurement systems, and if they are treated with respect;
Then they will do what needs to be done without being 'managed.'
It is the processes, the inert designs of work that need management and oversight, not people."

—Mike Hammer*

---

* Michael Hammer, *Beyond Reengineering: How the process-centered organization is changing our work and our lives*, Harper Business, 1997

How

1. Define and document new processes

In a product line siloed business there is a duplication of processes. Example, each silo has a sales force and customer service. Reorganize the corporate structure so that there is only one process for each function required. Each process will have a process engineer and a coach. See example below of Business Process & Communications Flow and Organizational Charts. After the initial implementation stabilizes, begin reengineering, combining and redefining the roles and tasks of each process for greater efficiencies.

2. Create a Business Strategy Process

The Business Strategy Process is the governance process for the organization.

3. Create Centers of Excellence (COE)

COEs are organized for uniformity on training and educating basic process skills.

4. Assign each person to a primary process and a COE.
5. Create a dual servant leadership model

Change managers roles to either a process engineer or coach depending on which they are best suited. New role definitions are below:

Process Engineer

- Define & monitor process metrics for throughput, productivity, cost and quality that balance the needs of Associates, Company and Customers.
- Teach and coach team members on the process
- Assess, monitor and evaluate performance on process tasks along with the coach

- Continue to analyze and communicate the current and future needs of the process
- Work with other process engineers and teams to align processes, resources and capital with the goals of Business Strategy
- Understand the PCO and be able to facilitate learning of the cultural system to all associates
- Develop actions to meet annual Business Roadmap and goals

Coach

- Know, Understand, Support & Assist the implementation of short-term & long-term business strategies for Associates
- Document problems and support resolutions of conflicts
- Hire, Assign & Separate Associates as Process Teams require
- Coach, Counsel, Support, Build Relationships, Inspire, Educate, Provide Training, Mentor and Discipline with input from Process Engineer
- Work with PEs and Associates to develop & monitor Individual Associate Development Plans (IADP) in conjunction with Business Strategy & Process Goals as defined by the IADP Process
- Continually work to support and improve understanding of Human Resources guidelines and compliance
- Understand the PCO and be able to facilitate learning of the cultural system to all associates
- Develop actions to meet annual Business Roadmap and goals

6. New titles for everyone in the organization become their Center of Excellence, Process. For example: a Customer

Service Representative title would become Customer Communications, Customer Service.

Business Process & Communications Flow

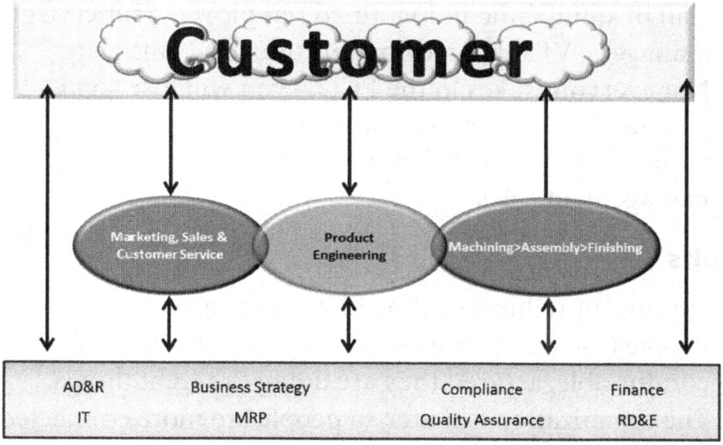

PCO Organizational Chart

Coach	Center of Excellence	Process	Process Engineer
	Administration	Associate Development & Resources	
		Finance / Compliance	
		Information Technology	
		MRP	
		Quality Assurance	
	Production	Machining	
		Assembly	
		Finishing	
	Customer Communication	Marketing	
		Sales	
		Customer Service	
	Engineering	Research, Development & Engineering	
		Product Engineering	
	Leadership	Business Strategy	
		Business	

Obstacles

1. Not "easy" to gain alignment and commitment around a PCO.
2. Takes a clear vision, time, perseverance and patience.
3. Can be quite difficult for "titled" employees (supervisors, managers, VPs) to give up their titles and authority.
4. Not everyone takes to the PCO—you will lose some people—by their choice and yours.
5. Some employees will feel they have lost their "ladder" to management roles

Results

1. Significant reduction of overhead expenses.
2. People (including management) just feel better, more comfortable, assured they are doing the right things.
3. The organization is flatter so people are more connected, take on more responsibilities and make better and faster decisions.
4. Because process engineer and coach leaders are no longer "managing" people, they have more time to:
   a. Work on process improvements
   b. Improve relationships
   c. Gain trust
   d. Train for the future
5. Quality improves – as people become more involved, they tend to fix problems rather than saying "he messed up, so I'll just let it go", as an example.
6. Reduce Costs: Without the trivial conflicts between employees, there is more time for doing productive work, resulting in fewer total employees and potentially fewer management staff.

Summary Results

BUSINESS METRICS

1. Improved profitability
   a. Reduced overhead costs with flatter organizational structure
   b. Lower material cost due to less scrap and better quality
   c. Lower production costs due to improved task skills
   d. More efficient processes – simplification
   e. More effective utilization of workforce
   f. Quicker recognition and response to bottlenecks and production problems
2. Continuous improvement
   a. Employee involvement
   b. Individual vertical and horizontal development
   c. Moving to the Work
3. Workflow
   a. Reduced late shipments
   b. Reduced expedite requests
   c. Fewer and focused projects completed
4. Traceable documentation for training and learning for ISO Compliance
5. Reduced turnover reducing cost of hiring, training and not having skills needed

CULTURE AND WORK ENVIRONMENT

1. A community of leaders
2. A trusting environment
3. Transparent compensation plans
4. Improved Teamwork

5. Willingness to move-to-the-work and learn new skills
6. Improved self-awareness and compassion for self and others
7. More effective communications
8. Everyone feels heard and acknowledged
9. More "us", less "we/them"
10. People take on more responsibilities and less afraid to make decisions.

LEADERSHIP

1. Improved Direction, alignment and commitment for all employees
2. Better decisions throughout organization - all levels
3. More time with 80% good and developing employees (not the 20% problems)
4. Without the constant, trivial conflicts brought to Leadership
    a. More time for doing productive work
    b. Reduced time for hiring and training new employees
    c. Fewer total employees, management and HR staff
5. Process engineers have more time to work on process improvements, develop metrics and train the process.
6. Coaches have more time to improve relationships, gain trust and develop employees by eliminating time spent on past performance

About the Authors

Loyal M. (Butch) Peterman, Jr. is President and Co-Founder of Abrasive Technology, Inc., a leading manufacturer of superabrasive grinding wheels and tools with 10 facilities around the world.

Butch is Director of Manufacturing with Heart, Inc., a consulting and coaching company for small manufacturing businesses. He is an executive coach and business consultant.

As the leader of Abrasive's long-term Business Strategy Team, he created a company with a positive and productive workplace based on unique organizational structure, early adopter of technologies, and culture centered on his core belief that "People Can be Trusted".

Butch holds BS and MS degrees in Mechanical Engineering from the University of Cincinnati, an MBA from Xavier University and is EQ and Denison Culture Survey certified. His career began at General Electric Aviation and GE Superabrasives before opening his own company. He also holds several global patents.

Butch enjoys connecting with people, engineering, making things simple, change, inventing, playing golf, the stock market, real estate investment, traveling, fine dining , wines & champagnes, learning, yoga, and meditation.

bpeterman@manufacturingwithheart.com
mobile: 1-614-571-8414

Tanya L. Patrella is President of Manufacturing with Heart, Inc., a consulting and coaching company for small manufacturing businesses. She is an executive coach and Human Resources consultant.

Tanya was an executive for Abrasive Technology, Inc., a worldwide manufacturer of superabrasive grinding wheels and tools. During her twenty-five years, she was Vice President of Administration, Marketing, Human Resources and coach for the global Leadership Team.

As an original member of Abrasive's long-term Business Strategy Team, Tanya has in-depth experience in Organizational and Leadership Development, Coaching Leadership Team Members as well as global business and compliance, project management, and acquisition integrations.

She holds a Bachelor Degree in Business Administration from Ohio State University and is certified in the Myers-Briggs Type Inventory (MBTI), FIRO-B, Denison Culture Survey and EQ assessments for improving self-awareness.

In addition to her corporate successes, Tanya loves helping others through career coaching people in transition—young folks just starting out or anyone in transition in careers or wanting to be!

She also enjoys gardening, reading, learning, yoga, meditation, time with her three sisters and two daughters, a good Oregon Pinot Noir, fine dining, and walking in the woods.

tpatrella@manufacturingwithheart.com
mobile: 1-614-571-8586

Tanya L. Patrella is President of Manufacturing [illegible] Heart, Inc., a consulting group coaching companies focused on manufacturing processes. She is an executive coach and Human [illegible] consultant.

Tanya was an executive for Abrasive Technology, Inc., worldwide manufacturers of [illegible] grinding wheels and tools. During her [illegible] years, she was Vice President of Administration, overseeing Human Resources and leading the global leadership team.

As an original member of Abrasive's [illegible] Strategy Team, Tanya has in-depth experience in organizational and leadership development, coaching, leadership team development, [illegible] business and continuous process management, and acquisition integration.

She holds a Master's Degree in Business Administration from Ohio State University and is certified in the Myers Briggs Type Indicator (MBTI), EQ-i, Denison culture survey, and [illegible] assessments for improving self-awareness.

In addition to her corporate success, Tanya loves helping others through [illegible] coaching people and mentoring young folks just starting out or anyone in transition in their career wanting to [illegible].

She also enjoys [illegible], reading, [illegible] with her [illegible] sisters and [illegible] good things, and [illegible] the world.

[illegible]heart.com
[illegible]